H3LT™ : The Hair Three-Legged-Table Solution for Education

H3LT™ : The Hair Three-Legged-Table Solution for Education

BEATRICE HAIR, MA. Ed.

Library of Congress Control Number: 2011907306
ISBN: Softcover   978-1-4628-6968-8
                 Ebook   978-1-4568-9358-3

H3LT: The Hair Three-Legged-Table Solution for Education is intended to inspire readers to seek tailor-made assistance for students. This book is a creative expression of the author's ideas. No part of *H3LT: The Hair Three-Legged-Table Solution for Education* is intended to offend any person, profession, culture, religion or country.

This book was printed in the United States of America.

To order additional copies of this book, contact:
Xlibris Corporation
1-888-795-4274
www.Xlibris.com
Orders@Xlibris.com
95292

Contents

Dedication

To my husband Randy Hair

Beatrice Hair, MA. Ed.

Founder and Director of Salisbury Tutoring Academy, Ltd.
The One-on-One School

Successful with thousands of students
A Revolutionary, Peaceful Solution for Education

Hair's Three-Legged-Table™ Behavior Modification Tool

Dr. Angelou offers Mrs. Hair

much success with her book H3LT™.

— Author Dr. Maya Angelou
Wake Forest University

Reviews

"*I have visited Beatrice Hair's Salisbury Tutoring Academy in Rowan County and was impressed with her success. We are pleased to have this dynamic, hands-on approach to education located in the Sixth District of North Carolina. I hope this book will assist parents as they seek answers to the educational needs of their children.*"

— Congressman Howard Coble

"*I believe the concepts and the theories Mrs. Hair professes are sound, deliberate, and functionally successful as is testified to by the number of students achieving amazing growth in language skills. We all know that learning to read is the key to learning everything else, so reading with comprehension is the greatest determiner of learning success. The personal testimonies of these parents, students, and teachers are the highest acclaim and the greatest predictor of success. I wish we could replicate this with every child in every school across America.*"

— General Rita Aragon

Former teacher, Principal, and College Instructor for the University of Oklahoma
Assistant to the Commander Air Education Training Command, USAF
Secretary Military and Veterans Affairs Oklahoma

"*Heartiest congratulations to Beatrice Hair on the publication of her first book. Parents and teachers, and most importantly, students with ADHD, will all benefit from the experience and expertise she shares in this book.*"

— Former U.S. Senator Elizabeth Dole

"I have co-taught with Beatrice in her workshops for teachers. She provides tools that work. Her approach is insightful and practical. She is energetic and connects with students and teachers alike."

— Jill Aiken, M.D.
Pediatrician

"The H3LT has brought peace to our home and has helped my sons' self-esteem soar. Even though my sons are seven years apart in age, the H3LT tool was equally effective in individually designing totally different programs. My younger son was struggling and is now a straight A student in his high school's honor program. Mrs. Hair makes changes to the H3LT to accommodate my son's needs and I highly recommend this tool as a solution for all students in America."

— Mr. and Mrs. Johnson
Salisbury Tutoring Academy

"Mrs. Hair's Three-Legged-Table has been successful for our family. Our high-school son has gone from feeling dispirited and like a failure, to feeling happy and enjoying school. The structure and consistency benefits teachers, parents and students. We are proud of our son's new-found success!"

— Dr. and Mrs. Gregory Scott
Salisbury Tutoring Academy

"Beatrice Hair has come up with some brilliant and creative ways to solve some major educational problems: holding the attention of children and effectively raising the performance of students at all levels, the poor performers and the average ones, as well as keeping the exceptional ones motivated."

— Drs. Eleanor and Woody Rowe
Authors

Special Appreciation

MANY THANKS ARE EXTENDED to those who are instrumental in the implementation of this behavior modification tool and in researching and writing *The Hair Three-Legged-Table Solution for Education.* I am grateful to every parent, student and teacher who has worked with me. They are the living proof that this tool is effective.

MY HEARTFELT APPRECIATION goes to the *Salisbury Tutoring Academy* staff. Our staff diligently maintains the integrity and consistency of this tool. It is an absolute honor to be an integral part of so many students' lives and their experience with transformational success.

MY FRIEND, **Patricia Hinson,** encouraged me to write this book. Appreciation with my deepest love is to my husband **Randy Hair** for the many years of emotional support—both in his affirmations and confirmations that helped fuel inspiration as the *Salisbury Tutoring Academy* was founded and developed. **Becky Smith**, a graduate school friend, volunteered her editing skills and humor. **Maria Fisher** oftentimes rendered much insight.

I am grateful to **Gina Pittard, M.D.**, for years of support and our special friendship. Thank you for the editing.

Thank you **Hélène Hinson Staley** for your editing gift.

My deepest wish is for this book to sanction a proven method for teachers, students and parents and transform those who are given an opportunity to use it.

Consultations

THE AUTHOR OF THIS book is available for consultations about the guidelines of *The Hair Three-Legged-Table*™ Behavior Modification Contract. To schedule a consultation with the author, contact the Academy at 1-(704)-633-8207. Sets of contracts are available for purchase by contacting the Academy.

> ➢ Hair's e-mail: *staltd@vnet.net*

> ➢ Salisbury Tutoring Academy school's website: *www.staltd.com.*

> ➢ Salisbury Tutoring Academy fax: 1-(704)-633-8206.

Hair's Behavior Modification Contract for:_____

DATES

GOALS								

Weekly Treats Include: _____

Completed Contract Treats Include: _____

You May Miss ___ Stickers per Contract

You May Miss ___ Contracts

Teacher: _____

Student: _____

Parent: _____

Foreword

WHAT DO STUDENTS NEED? They crave structure, consistency and individual attention.

> ➢ *What do classroom teachers need?*

  • They need uninterrupted instructional time and the ability to conserve their valuable energy.

> ➢ *What do parents need?*

  • They need support for their parenting efforts and a diplomatic understanding that stems from knowing their role.

THIS BOOK IS DESIGNED to address the challenges of all dilemmas and equip teachers and parents with a tool to create an accommodating educational environment for students to experience transformational changes. This tool commands the students' attention; then it keeps them motivated.

Introduction

"Never discourage anyone . . . who continuously makes progress, no matter how slow."

— Plato

TEACHERS AND PARENTS are frustrated when a student fails to realize his or her full potential. Academically, America's students are falling behind students in many countries. In parent-teacher conferences, both parties complain about the student without establishing a game plan to improve the situation.

THIS BOOK IS DESIGNED to accomplish several goals. It offers teachers and parents a powerful tool that has been used successfully with thousands of students in Salisbury, North Carolina. Using this tool, teachers, parents and students work together to BUILD PLATFORMS for powerful transformations. When a transformation occurs, the original problems disappear. A transformation is a light-bulb experience, which all teachers witness as they occur in the classroom. However, random light-bulbs are simply not enough. With careful program design, light-bulbs are created consistently. Teachers and parents learn how to design a BEHAVIOR MODIFICATION CONTRACT that features up to six individual goals. Teachers develop effective contracts for students that include collaboratively developed time frames, incentives and consequences.

This book is useful for helping students of all ages. It provides examples of age-appropriate contracts, journals and visual aids that facilitate learning for parents, students and teachers. The contracts command the students' attention and help to keep them motivated.

The contracts are effective with high-level, moderate-level and low-level achieving students. The goal is for students to experience a complete transformation of old behaviors and habits.

A boy named Trevor exemplifies the success of this program. When he came to us at the Salisbury Tutoring Academy, Trevor was a low-functioning student in the learning-disabled group. After four months of *The Hair Three-Legged-Table*™ *(H3LT)* program, Trevor achieved a remarkable transformation. He then transferred into the gifted program, became a straight "A" student, and even won his school's spelling bee! His miserable elementary years ended with great success.

North Carolina resident 16-year-old William was victimized by bullies and further harmed by indifferent teachers. He was struggling in school. Thanks to the *H3LT*™ program, he was totally transformed. Instead of failing math, William attained the highest average in his class. His newfound confidence shielded him from unsupportive teachers and cruel peers. He accomplished the goals we set for him: better study skills, an improved math skill set, and well-organized notes.

Overview

The intended audience of this book is teachers, parents and students who want to work as a team to develop agreed-upon goals and have those goals achieved and celebrated. It is a tool that can be used in many different ways at school, at home or by a tutor. Parents and teachers must be in a problem-solving mode for this to work.

The purpose of the contract is to teach a positive way to help modify student behavior and habits.

This how-to book's main tool is a chart that combines powerful incentive and consequence philosophies.

Teachers and parents using this book need to work as a team for the best interest of the student. Teachers and parents will lead the student out of a frustrating situation and into a positive problem-solving realm.

Teachers and parents will begin a healing process for themselves and the student(s) involved.

This how-to book's goal is for teachers and parents to learn skills that will help transform student behavior and habits. Teachers and parents will use a behavior modification tool to monitor and reward positive changes in student behavior; consequences will be used when needed.

Journal Prompts

THE FOLLOWING JOURNAL PAGES are for parents and/ or teachers to sort out their natural emotional state and move into an effective, objective problem-solving mode. Write some of your educational concerns from your unique perspective.

START BY DESCRIBING the risks to students when parents and teachers do not work together as a team.

Examples of journal entries include:

1. Students do not know whom to respect when teachers and parents are not communicating in a positive way.
2. Students who do not achieve their potential could become adults who do not reach their potential.
3. Constant conflict can cause emotional scars.
4.
5.
6.
7.
8.

Now you should have a clear sense of why you want to learn how to use *The Hair Contract*©.

Instructional Strategies & Rationale

T HERE ARE NO QUICK fixes when it comes to education. Teachers should expect student behavior to modify slowly over time. The question: *"What should I do with this child?"* will be answered. The North Carolina Department of Public Instruction states that teachers are responsible for teaching all their students. This is mandated by the federal standard (NCDPI, 2011). Not only must students be taught, they must also be stopped from disrupting the education of others.

Getting Started: Incentives

TEACHERS AND PARENTS MUST take into account that students need structure, academic modification and behavior modification. Up front, everyone must understand the goals and how they will be measured.

MANY STUDENTS KNOW WHAT they want in terms of incentives. The first step is to sit down with the student and request a WISH LIST. At this point, the teacher's role becomes that of the student's advocate and ally. The next step is for the teacher to schedule a POWER MEETING with the parents and negotiate for the student's incentives. A principal or guidance counselor may also assume this role of scheduling and mediating.

HERE ARE SOME EXAMPLES of incentives; they can be used to help the student brainstorm ideas for a wish list:

- Trip to theme park with a friend

- Sleep-over

- Digital games (*Give them things they like!*)

- Movies

- Special dinner at favorite restaurant with family, friends or both

- Allowance

- Music CD or downloads

- Special privileges (*At the high school level this may involve car privileges or parts.*)

- Special trip to mountains, beach or athletic event

- Fishing trip with Dad (*Attention is always a good incentive!*)

- For high school students: later curfews, a car, accessories for the car, etc.

- Manicure, pedicure, massage or facial

Getting Started: Consequences

CONSEQUENCES MAY BE ANYTHING teachers or parents can use as leverage. For example, one middle school student lost the privilege of wearing his favorite shoes to school. For high school students, weekend driving and curfew privileges can be curtailed. Access to electronics can be denied.

Consequences should be reasonable and consistent:

- LOSS OF PRIVILEGES — These must be specific: No television for one day; no electronics for one day, no phone, no music, etc.

- NO ALLOWANCE — The students may owe by subtracting money for missed goals. For example, students can earn $1 for an achieved goal, and they would lose $2 per missed goal. (*To further clarify-A student may potentially earn $6 per week for achieving six goals. If the student misses one goal, $2 is subtracted from the potential $6 for a reduced total of $4.*) It is recommended that colorful markers or stickers be used to symbolize accomplished goals on the contract, and X's be used to denote missed goals.

- EXTRA HOUSEHOLD CHORES — With this consequence, students usually decide for themselves that they would rather meet the academic goals than do extra chores. Chore ideas may include: cleaning cars, washing windows, scrubbing bathrooms, raking leaves, washing dishes, etc.

Getting Started: The Up-Front Power Meeting

THE PURPOSE OF THE UP-FRONT POWER MEETING is to save time in the long run. This is where *The Hair Three-Legged-Table*™ philosophy is conveyed and negotiations begin. In order to conduct an effective parent / teacher / student conference, teachers and parents may use the following as a checklist:

❑ Consequences need to be reasonable, specific and loving.

❑ Consequences should not be overwhelming. Force and pressure causes the paralysis of growth. For example, one missed goal should result in one day of no electronics, rather than a week.

❑ Allow a designated number of missed goals (i.e. three missed goals in an eight-week period) without any consequences to allow a child to be a child. Remember that there are six goals during an eight-week period of time.

❑ There is a fine line between holding a standard and being overbearing. Misses must be allowed matter-of-factly without parents *"bearing down"* on the students.

❑ Do not over-punish or under-punish. Many parents ignore behaviors for too long and then explode and become over-reactive.

❑ Offer positive incentives with consistency.

❑ Incentives must be offered on time because children do not understand excuses. As an analogy, an employer cannot explain that an employee's paycheck is not ready because the employer's grandmother is in the hospital.

❑ Do not give incentives early. Again, if an employer offers an employee his/her paycheck early, it may lessen motivation.

❑ The contract operates on this paycheck basis. As adults, even if we love our jobs, we could easily find other things we would rather do with our time. A paycheck motivates us to stay committed, just as the incentive motivates students to stay focused on the contract goals.

❑ Incentives help provide healing to psychic wounds; often students have been hurting for years.

❑ Make the first incentive especially inviting to the student to help the student buy into the solution more quickly. Be sure to refer to their list. Example: ski trip, shopping spree or a new outfit.

❑ Parents need to use caution in offering incentives. The incentive must be an item that is available in stores, in season, etc., so that it will be delivered on time.

❑ Parents should **give** their children **less** material goods and privileges to allow them to **earn more** instead.

❑ Parents, students and teachers need to agree and sign the contract. This way each member of The Three-Legged-Table™ Contract commits to being a part of the solution.

❑ Many students need to have customized, individualized instruction. This tool can be used for that purpose.

❑ Parents must coordinate with grandparents, spouses, ex-spouses or significant others to explain the agreement and avoid misinterpretation of the incentive understanding. For example, other family members should not inadvertently give the contracted incentive to the student as a birthday present or for another occasion.

❑ Parents need to provide additional praise when students receive all their stickers.

❑ Parents should not over-punish by *"throwing away the big stick."* For example, instead of not allowing a child to play sports for the whole season, have the privilege of playing weekly games to be earned on a weekly basis.

Getting Started: What to do When Parental Support is Missing

In CASES WHERE CLASSROOM teachers are not able to count on parents for consistent incentives, teachers can create their own incentive system:

1) Homework passes

2) Extra recess time with another class

3) Candy (*caution concerning obesity or other health issues*)

4) Gift certificates to a place to which they have access

5) Anything that will give students extra attention or *"limelight recognition"* (Student-of-the-Month or the privilege of passing out papers)

6) An extra trip to the treasure box

Possible consequences if there is no parental support:

1) Loss of recess or free time (Build in an extra recess class to use as leverage.)

2) Extra assignments

3) Loss of any classroom privileges for the next day

4) Sentence writing

Getting Started: A Positive Tone

THE GOALS SHOULD BE worded in a positive way. For example, instead of saying, *"No hitting your neighbor,"* one might say, *"Show kindness to your neighbor."* The writing style is an important component of the contract's success. This emphasizes the idea of making lifestyle changes and seeing goodness as a way of being. Positive wording is much more effective and sets the contract's tone. Examples include:

➤ Negative — No hitting your neighbor. *vs.* Positive — Show kindness to your neighbor. (Children ages four-five are allowed one verbal warning.)

➤ Negative—No back-talking. *vs.* Positive—Speak respectfully to others.

➤ Negative — No ignoring verbal requests. *vs.* Positive — Follow directions before countdown is over (can be ascending or descending one-two-three or three-two-one).

➤ Negative — Do not wait until the last minute to study for your test. *vs.* Positive — Study flashcards five days a week.

"Retros"
Earning Goals
Retroactively
Under Special
Circumstances

U SUALLY, EACH WEEK'S GOALS stand alone. Earning goals retroactively allows students to earn back a goal they missed through no fault of their own. This means a student can earn back the sticker retroactively the next time the contract is checked. We coin these as *"Retros."* For example, a student may state,

"I got my homework agenda signed by my teachers, but I left it in the car which went to the shop."

In this case, the student receives an *"R"* instead of a sticker and will have to furnish the homework agenda the next time he and his teacher update the contract. We usually give credit for that week only. In this case, his goals will be retroactively checked for the previous week.

Summary Pointers

TEACHERS AND PARENTS WILL need to keep the following concepts in mind before designing their behavior modification tool:

- The behavior modification tool can be used in many different ways for home, school or with a tutor.

- Eight weeks is a reasonable time period for an incentive. When using this tool with children under the age of six, an incentive every four weeks works best.

- Allow a minimum of three and a maximum of eight misses per every eight weeks.

- The tool can be used with a daily incentive, such as allowance for a middle school student. Remember to subtract money for misses.

- It can be used with a long-term goal. For example, a high school student would successfully complete eight contracts to earn a car.

- It can be checked-off daily or be done once a week.

- Giving additional praise with stickers is vital.

- Colorful stickers or checkmarks help. Xs should be used to denote misses. The X's in the contract work as visual reminders to motivate students. (It serves as an alert that behavior must change.)

- When a student misses a goal, the emphasis must be on the changes to be made. For example, a teacher points out, *"Johnny, you missed your goal of speaking respectfully to others this week."* (He back-talked.) *"What can you do to reach your goal next week?"* The student must vocalize the exact change he is willing to commit to.

- *"Not Applicable"* or *"NA"* can be used when a goal does not apply one week or if there is a goal that needs to begin a few weeks later.

Final Journaling

W HEN THE HAIR CONTRACT© IS COMPLETED, teachers and parents will be able to incorporate *The Hair Three-Legged-Table*™ philosophy for successful behavior modification specific to each student. Conducting an effective power meeting for all three parties is crucial. Journal notes need to include what was most effective and ineffective about different power meetings. It is also important to document what types of incentives worked for different types of students. These journal entries can be used as references over time.

As you are going along and re-adjusting contract goals, write what worked and what did not work about your Up-Front Power Meeting. What changes will you make next time?

 What was effective about your Up-Front Power Meeting?

 What was missing from your Up-Front Power Meeting?

(There will always be something forgotten. Just document and refer to notes before the next power meeting.)

In this part of the journal, write incentive and consequence ideas. Use your own ideas as well as ours. Each time you draw up a new contract, you will have these ideas at hand.

40

 **Effective Incentives**

Effective Consequences

Ineffective Incentives

Ineffective Consequences

How do you know that the goals, incentives and consequences are effective? They work! If the student misses three or less goals in an eight-week period of time, and the behavior improves on the six issues listed, you have success. When old issues become obsolete, it is time to write new goals.

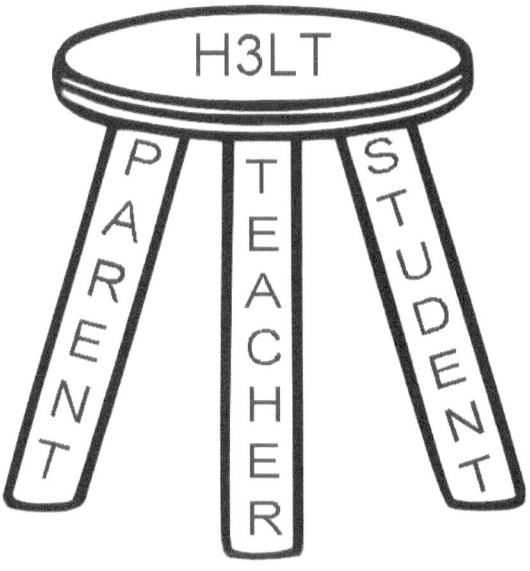

In Review: Five Success Steps

AFTER FILLING THE JOURNAL OUT, you will have a record that includes what incentives and consequences work, as well as what has not worked. Be sure to build on this as you learn to utilize this tool.

- Step 1: Write a list of reasons why the student's behavior and habits need to be addressed.

- Step 2: List six major goals for the student in the journal space provided.

- Step 3: Design a contract specific to the student's needs.

- Step 4: Conduct The Up-Front Power Meeting and secure commitments and signatures.

- Step 5: Maintain consistency.

Hair's Behavior Modification Contract for:_____

	DATES							
GOALS								

Weekly Treats Include: _____

Completed Contract Treats Include: _____

You May Miss ___ Stickers per Contract

You May Miss ___ Contracts

Teacher: _____

Student: _____

Parent: _____

Practical Application

D ESCRIBE THE TOP SIX negative behaviors or issues each student is experiencing. Summarize with written goals. For example: *"Johnny is never ready for tests, and he has panic attacks at the last minute."*

Goal: Study flashcards five days a week.

First Student _____

1. **Issue:**
   Goal:
2. **Issue:**
   Goal:
3. **Issue:**
   Goal:
4. **Issue:**
   Goal:
5. **Issue:**
   Goal:
6. **Issue:**
   Goal:

Second Student _____

1. **Issue:**
   Goal:
2. **Issue:**
   Goal:
3. **Issue:**
   Goal:
4. **Issue:**
   Goal:
5. **Issue:**
   Goal:
6. **Issue:**
   Goal:

Third Student_____

1. **Issue:**
   Goal:
2. **Issue:**
   Goal:
3. **Issue:**
   Goal:
4. **Issue:**
   Goal:
5. **Issue:**
   Goal:
6. **Issue:**
   Goal:

THIS CONTRACT CAN BE used to motivate a brilliant student, to help a low-achieving student, and with students of all ages.

Problem: Johnny is a middle school student who does not bring materials to class. He interrupts others, does not do his homework and often lays his head on his desk during class. He has trouble with math because he does not know his multiplication facts yet.

Solution: Read the following contract with these issues addressed by goals.

Sample Contract

Hair's Behavior Modification Contract for: *Johnny*

	DATES							
GOALS								
Bring materials								
Raise hand and wait to speak								
Know math fact cards								
Keep head up during class								
Bring completed homework								

Weekly Treats Include: *Allowance + 1 dollar per goal -2 per miss*

Completed Contract Treats Include: *Ski trip after 3 contracts!*

You May Miss __3__ Stickers per Contract   *Consequence per miss - one day of no T.V.*

You May Miss ___ Contracts

Teacher: _____

Student: _____

Parent: _____

Copyrighted 1997
Salisbury Tutoring Academy

Hair's Behavior Modification Contract for:_____

GOALS	DATES							

Weekly Treats Include: _____

Completed Contract Treats Include: _____

You May Miss ___ Stickers per Contract

You May Miss ___ Contracts

Teacher: _____

Student: _____

Parent: _____

Hair's Behavior Modification Contract for:_____

GOALS	DATES							

Weekly Treats Include: _____

Completed Contract Treats Include: _____

You May Miss ___ Stickers per Contract

You May Miss ___ Contracts

Teacher: _____

Student: _____

Parent: _____

Copyrighted 1997, 2011
Salisbury Tutoring Academy

Final Check-In

Do YOU KNOW HOW to list student issues, negotiate *an Up-Front Power Meeting*, word the goals, follow through consistently, provide incentives and consequences and assess whether the goals were accomplished? Has the student experienced a transformation? Did the contract achieve the desired goals? Congratulations. Now, please spread the word to help as many students as possible experience the magic of this powerful tool!

Questions & Answers

WHAT WILL TEACHERS AND PARENTS LEARN?

Teachers and parents will learn how to use The Hair Three-Legged-Table™ Behavior Modification Contract.

Teachers and parents will be able to individually apply this contract to different students.

THIS BOOK FEATURES THREE techniques: cognitive, psychomotor and affective. The contract is adapted to the individual student's needs and aptitudes. The student will transform negative habits into productive ones.

This contract (based on The Hair Three-Legged-Table™ system) requires supportive roles from teachers and parents. Initially, students tend to be motivated by incentives and consequences alone. Once a student experiences some success, more cooperation ensues. This system presumes that if one leg of The Hair Three-Legged-Table™ is broken or weak, the table, together with its performance measurement, will not stand. Parents, teachers, and students need to follow through on their individual responsibilities. This approach virtually guarantees the success of the contract, providing all those who sign it honor their commitment.

Some often-asked questions:

1. **Why is the performance measurement method effective?**

   Students crave structure, individual attention and consistency.

2. **What is the advantage and disadvantage of this measurement method?**

   The advantage: Students can observe hard work paying off. The disadvantage: Without a strong commitment from all three parties, the contract will not be successful. All three parties must work together, and all parties must understand their respective, separate roles.

3. **Who should care about the results of performance measurements?**

   Everyone will benefit from the results of performance measurement if the contract is successfully fulfilled. Students receive incentives and feelings of accomplishment. Teachers enjoy a more positive teaching climate. Parents receive support while trying to raise a responsible citizen and family member. The healing process begins for everyone, and the stage is set for transformation.

4. **Why should teachers, students and parents care?**

   TEACHERS have less stress when they deal with motivated students. Classroom teachers have limited time to deal individually with negative behaviors and attitudes during instruction. The contract helps teachers to be more effective and efficient. Once the contract is implemented, checking it off can often take less than a minute.

STUDENTS are proud of their accomplishments; they experience improved self-esteem. They enjoy their teacher's guaranteed individual attention. The stage is set for transformation to occur.

PARENTS gratefully observe improved behavior and increased academic success. They see a powerful transformation in their child, who finds more pleasure in learning.

Sources

North Carolina Department of Public Instruction. (2011). North Carolina Adopts Common Core State Standards. P. 1. Retrieved on January 22, 2011, from
http://www.ncpublicschools.org/newsroom/news/2009-10/20100604-01

Rothwell, W., Kazanas, H.C., Palloff, R.M., Pratt, K., Smith, P.L., & Ragan, T.J. (2002).
Instructional Design. [University of Phoenix Custom Edition eBook]. New York: John Wiley & Sons.

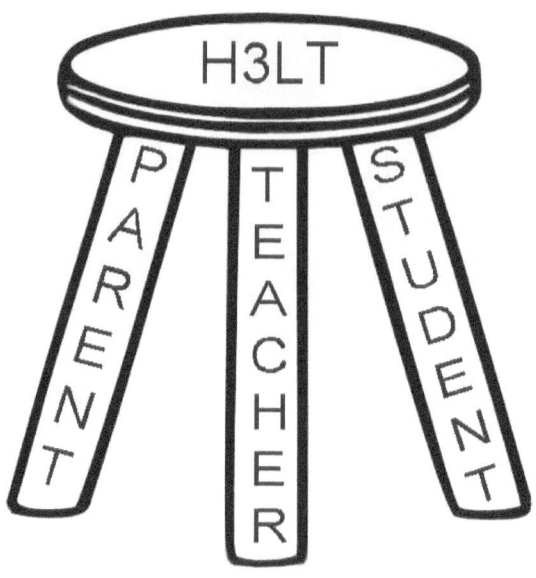

BEATRICE R.D. HAIR, MA. Ed. is an award-winning entrepreneur and teacher. She has worked 23 years with students, both as a teacher and as a business owner. She has a Bachelor of Arts degree in Education from Wake Forest University and holds a Masters of Education concentrating on Curriculum and Instruction from the University of Phoenix. After eight years as a public school teacher, Beatrice founded *Salisbury Tutoring Academy, Ltd. The One-on-One School.* She has won many awards as an entrepreneur and teacher. Beatrice Hair was featured on multiple North Carolina news networks including: Fox News Rising, and evening news with WGHP, WSOC and Channel 14.

PARENTS OFTEN BLAME TEACHERS, themselves and their child when a student is not achieving his/her potential. Conversely, some teachers blame parents for being resigned and not positively participating in their child's education. While this is transpiring, students are falling behind in many subject areas. The academic progress of American students now significantly lags behind that of other countries. Thousands of students have been successful using the tool outlined in this book. This powerful tool, H3LT™, can be applied to all types of students at any age.

Book Summary: What do students need? They crave structure, consistency and individual attention. What do classroom teachers need? They need uninterrupted instructional time and the ability to conserve their valuable energy. What do parents need? They need support for their parenting efforts and a peaceful understanding that stems from knowing their role. This book is designed to address the challenges of all dilemmas and equip teachers and parents with tools to create an accommodating educational environment for these students to experience transformational changes. This H3LT™ tool commands the students' attention, and then it keeps them motivated.

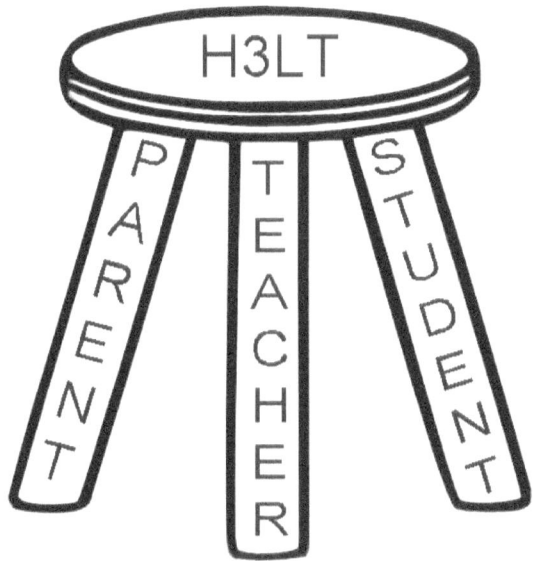

Beatrice R.D. Hair Biography

BEATRICE R.D. HAIR, MA. Ed. dedicates her life to child advocacy. She is the founder and owner of the *Salisbury Tutoring Academy, Ltd. the One-on-One School*, which is a franchised tutoring academy for ages four-to-adult. She was awarded the title of *U.S. Small Business Administration 2010 North Carolina Small Business Person of the Year.* She received a *Congressional Recognition Award* from Congressman Howard Coble for her work in April of 2010. In May of 2010, she was personally congratulated by U.S. President Barrack Obama at the White House in Washington, D.C. Her work successes were featured on multiple North Carolina news networks including: Fox News Rising, evening news with WGHP, WSOC and

Channel 14. She is the nationally televised Icon (NBC, ABC, CBS, etc.) for the University of Phoenix's School of Education for 2011. She has appeared in the Huffington Post, the New Yorker magazine and thousands of on-line ads throughout the internet.

BEATRICE HAIR'S TECHNOLOGY HELPS top students become competitive for scholarships, moderate-level students become high achievers, and low-achieving students become high-functioning students. Her franchise also provides all students one-on-one attention.

Hair's academy offers long-range educational tutoring programs designed to help students gain acceptance to their colleges of choice with scholarships by helping increase SAT scores, dealing with Attention Deficit Disorders issues, boosting grades, dealing with learning disabilities, increasing reading competency and enriching unchallenged minds.

Hair designed the programs for her academy which is a brick-and-mortar school. Hair's staff uses her tools to implement each student's individualized tutoring design. Thousands of students have experienced success with the structure and philosophy of this model. She has franchised her business and is committed to the success of *Salisbury Tutoring Academy's* anywhere.

One of the academy's student success stories was featured on the cover of the *Phoenix Focus Magazine (600,000 subscribers)*. Mrs. Hair's success as a business innovator was featured in *The Salisbury Post, Rowan Business Magazine, Charlotte Business Journal,* the *Wake Forest Magazine* and *Women Entrepreneur Magazine.*

She is a graduate of Wake Forest University (1987), where she earned a Bachelor of Arts in Education with a minor in Health and Sports Science. She has a Masters of Education in Curriculum and Instruction from the University of Phoenix (2004). She has over 23 years of education experience.

www.ingramcontent.com/pod-product-compliance
Lightning Source LLC
Chambersburg PA
CBHW031329290526
45784CB00014B/2444